Brad B

The B

Bloomsbury Methuen Drama
An imprint of Bloomsbury Publishing Plc

B L O O M S B U R Y
LONDON · OXFORD · NEW YORK · NEW DELHI · SYDNEY

Bloomsbury Methuen Drama

An imprint of Bloomsbury Publishing Plc

Imprint previously known as Methuen Drama

50 Bedford Square	1385 Broadway
London	New York
WC1B 3DP	NY 10018
UK	USA

www.bloomsbury.com

Bloomsbury is a registered trade mark of Bloomsbury Publishing Plc

First published 2016

© Brad Birch, 2016

Brad Birch has asserted his right under the Copyright, Designs
and Patents Act, 1988, to be identified as author of this work.

British Library Cataloguing-in-Publication Data
A catalogue record for this book is available from the British Library.

ISBN: PB: 978-1-3500-0133-6
ePub: 978-1-3500-0134-3
ePDF: 978-1-3500-0135-0

Library of Congress Cataloging-in-Publication Data
A catalog record for this book is available from the Library of Congress.

Typeset by Mark Heslington Ltd, Scarborough, North Yorkshire
Printed and bound in Great Britain

A co-production between the Orange Tree Theatre,
W14 Productions and Theatre Bench,
in association with the National Theatre Studio:
The J.P. Morgan Award for Emerging Directors production

The Brink
A NEW PLAY BY BRAD BIRCH

Jo **ALICE HAIG**
Martin/Mr Boyd **VINCE LEIGH**
Chloe/Jessica **SHVORNE MARKS**
Nick **CIARÁN OWENS**

Director **MEL HILLYARD**
Designer **HYEMI SHIN**
Lighting Designer **LIZZIE POWELL**
Sound Designer & Composer **TOM GIBBONS**
Movement Director **CAROLINA VALDÉS**
Costume Supervisor **HOLLY ROSE HENSHAW**
Casting Consultant **CHARLOTTE BEVAN**

Production Manager **STUART BURGESS**
Production Technician **TJ CHAPPELL**
Stage Manager **EVE KERR**
Deputy Stage Manager **AMY SLATER**
Assistant Stage Manager **LUIS HENSON**

Thanks to Rachael Williams

The first performance of *The Brink* © Brad Birch
was at the Orange Tree Theatre on 7 April 2016

J.P.Morgan

National Theatre Studio

The National Theatre is dedicated to making the very best theatre and sharing it with as many people as possible. They produce up to 30 productions on the South Bank each year, ranging from re-imagined classics — such as Greek tragedy and Shakespeare — to modern masterpieces and new work by contemporary writers and theatre-makers. The work they make strives to be as open, as diverse, as collaborative and as national as possible. The NT wants to inspire artists and audiences to think in new ways, to constantly re-imagine the act of making theatre. The newly formed New Work Department is housed at the NT Studio and brings together the combined resource of the Literary Department and the Studio into an engine room for the development of new work for all the National Theatre's stages and beyond; they are committed to nurturing innovative work from new writers, directors, creative artists and performers.

The National Theatre is supported by Arts Council England. The Emerging Director's Award is supported by J.P. Morgan.

Supported using public funding by **ARTS COUNCIL ENGLAND**   **J.P.Morgan**

W14 Productions

W14 Productions is run by Annabel Williamson. Recent W14 Productions include *The Late Henry Moss, Upper Cut* and *As You Like It* at Southwark Playhouse and Annabel produced (in her own name) the initial run of *Beyond Caring* at The Yard. Annabel is a Stage One Bursary recipient (2014).

@W14Productions

Jim Zalles launched Theatre Bench in October 2012 to support the development of new works in theatre and dance. Recent productions include *Teddy* and *These Trees are Made of Blood* (Southwark Playhouse), *Claustrophobia* (The Hope), Carthage and *Thérèse Raquin* (Finborough), *Our Friends The Enemy* (Edinburgh Festival), *LIFT* (Soho) and *Drunk* (Bridewell).

@TheatreBench

The Orange Tree Theatre aims to stir, delight, challenge, move and amaze with a bold and continually evolving mix of new and rediscovered plays in our unique in-the-round space. We want to change lives by telling remarkable stories from a wide variety of times and places, filtered through the singular imagination of our writers and the remarkable close-up presence of our actors.

A theatre of this scale, with the audience wrapped around the players, invites acting to be the centre of the experience. This is theatre as a figurative art: the human being literally at its centre. We want to experience voices and stories from our past and our present alongside visions of the future. Life as it's lived: unplugged and unmiked. Close-up magic. Truths the hand can touch.

Over its forty-five-year history the Orange Tree has had a very strong track record in discovering writers and promoting their early work, as well as rediscovering artists from the past whose work had either been disregarded or forgotten. Over the past eighteen months the work of Terence Rattigan, Robert Holman, Doris Lessing, Mustapha Matura, Bernard Shaw, Sharman Macdonald and D.H. Lawrence has played alongside new work by Alistair McDowall, Alice Birch, Deborah Bruce, Chris Urch and Adam Barnard.

Orange Tree Theatre

COMING SOON

12 MAY – 25 JUNE

The Philanderer
BY BERNARD SHAW

30 JUNE – 30 JULY

French Without Tears
BY TERENCE RATTIGAN

OCT 2016

Blue Heart
BY CARYL CHURCHILL
Booking opens in May

orangetreetheatre.co.uk
020 8940 3633

Artistic Director **Paul Miller** Executive Director **Sarah Nicholson**

The OT is a registered charity (266128) and would like to thank the London Borough of Richmond-upon-Thames, RPLC, Hampton Fuel Allotment Charity, David & Selina Marks, the Devey family, the Haskel Family Foundation, the J Paul Getty Jnr Charitable Trust, the Kew Fete Committee and our dedicated Members for their generous support.

For more information about supporting the OT see **orangetreetheatre.co.uk**

ALICE HAIG
Jo

Alice trained at Webber Douglas Academy of Dramatic Art and Central School of Speech and Drama.

Theatre credits include: *Baby* (Hope); *84 Charing Cross Road* (Southwark Playhouse); *'Tis Pity She's a Whore, Holding Fire!* (Shakespeare's Globe); *Sense and Sensibility* (Watermill, Newbury); *Wasted* (Paines Plough); *Descent* (Southwark Playhouse); *I Didn't Always Live Here* (Finborough); *The Fairy Queen* (Glyndebourne); *Hard Shoulders* (Pleasance); *Even Stillness Breathes Softly Against a Brick Wall, What Cheryl Did Next, Greek Tragedy* (Theatre503); *Table for 6* (TenFour Theatre); *As You Like It, Hay Fever* (West Yorkshire Playhouse); *The Curse of the Starving Class* (Royal Lyceum); *When Cheryl Was Brassic* (nabokov); *The Children's Hour* (Royal Exchange).

TV includes: *Brutality, Scottish Killers*.

VINCE LEIGH
Martin/Mr Boyd

Theatre credits include: *Sunny Afternoon* (Hampstead/West End); *The Taming of the Shrew, Twelfth Night, Henry V, The Winter's Tale, Pocket Dream, A Midsummer Night's Dream, Rose Rage* (Propeller); *A Funny Thing Happened on the Way to the Forum* (National Theatre); *The Winter's Tale* (Headlong); *Is There Life After High School* (Bridewell); *Henry VIII, The Spanish Tragedy, Cymbeline, Much Ado About Nothing* and *Julius Caesar* (RSC); *Dead Guilty, The Fly, Maxwell, Cats* (West End); *Othello* (Watermill, Newbury/Tokyo); *Lysistrata* (Richmond/Greece); *Moll Flanders* (Lyric Hammersmith); *Ten Commandments* (The Place); *Tutankhamun* (Imagination); *Just So* (Tricycle/West End); *PVT Wars* (Finborough); *No Remission* (Edinburgh Festival).

TV includes: *Babylon, Endeavour, New Tricks, A Touch of Frost, Trial and Retribution, Silent Witness, Waking the Dead, Miss Marple, Family Affairs, Jonathan Creek, Broken Heart, Jo Brand: Through the Cakehole, One Foot in the Grave*.

Films include *Shadow Man, Oscar's Date, Passing Through, That Sunday*.

SHVORNE MARKS
Chloe/Jessica

Shvorne trained at Arts Ed.

Theatre credits include: *Flare Path* (UK tour); *Macbeth* (Orange Tree); *The Witch of Edmonton* (RSC); *The Tea Party* (Park); *Some Other Mother* (Traverse); *Home* (The Last Refuge); *Trust Fund* (Bush); *Seasoned* (The Tobacco Factory)

TV includes: *Endeavour* (series II and III), *Holby City*.

Audio includes: *Dr Who* (BBC); *DNA* (Listening Books); *Bridge to the Wounded Heart* (Gap Digital).

CIARÁN OWENS
Nick

Ciarán trained at LAMDA.

Theatre credits include: *Disco Pigs* (House); *So Here We Are* (Royal Exchange/Hightide); *The Crocodile* (Invisible Dot/Manchester International Festival); *King John* (Shakespeare's Globe); *A Handful of Stars* (Theatre503/Trafalgar Studios); *Oh What a Lovely War* (Theatre Royal Stratford East); *Candide, Titus Andronicus, A Mad World My Masters* (RSC); *Our Country's Good* (Out of Joint); *Mercury Fur* (Old Red Lion/Trafalgar Studios); *A Butcher of Distinction* (King's Head).

TV includes: *Arthur and George, Spotless, Wallander, The Inbetweeners*.

BRAD BIRCH
Writer

Brad Birch is the 2016 recipient of the Harold Pinter Commission at the Royal Court.

His plays include: *The Endless Ocean* (RWCMD); *Selfie* (NYT); *Tender Bolus* (Royal Exchange); *Gardening for the Unfulfilled and Alienated* (Undeb Theatre, winner of a Scotsman Edinburgh Fringe First 2013); *Even Stillness Breathes Softly Against A Brick Wall* (Theatre503/Soho); *Where the Shot Rabbits Lay* (Royal Court/White Bear); *Light Arrested Between the Curtain and the Glass* (Sherman Cymru).

MEL HILLYARD
Director

Mel is the receipient of the J.P. Morgan Award for Emerging Directors as part of which she has been Resident Director at the National Theatre Studio.

Directing credits include: *The Late Henry Moss* (Southwark Playhouse); *Love and Information* (Caird Studio/RWCMD); *Hamlet* (The Secret Nuclear Bunker - East 15); *Hard Shoulders* (Latitude); *Even Stillness Breathes Softly Against a Brick Wall* (Theatre503); *In an Instant* (Latitude Festival/Theatre503); *His Face Her Face, Three Is Company* (King's Head); *Loose Ends* (Edinburgh Festival). She has also acted as Associate, Assistant or Staff Director at the National Theatre, RSC, Hampstead, West End and Theatre Royal Stratford East.

HYEMI SHIN
Designer
Hyemi was a winner of the Linbury Prize for Stage Design 2011.

Designs include: *A Midsummer Night's Dream, Morning, Desire Under the Elms* (costume design), *Secret Theatre, Herons* (Lyric Hammersmith); *Sizwe Banzi is Dead, Dirty Butterfly* (Young Vic); *Viriditas, No 1 Convergence* (Rambert); *Life's Witness* (Linbury Studio Theatre); *Unearth* (The National Ballet of Canada).

LIZZIE POWELL
Lighting Designer
Lizzie trained at London Academy of Music and Dramatic Arts.

Her lighting designs include: *The Fruit Trilogy* (West Yorkshire Playhouse); *Endgame, The Choir, Fever dream: Southside, A Christmas Carol, The Libertine, Far Away, Seagulls, Krapp's Last Tape, Footfalls* (Citizens Theatre); *Romeo & Juliet* (Crucible); *Violence and Son, Weekly Rep* (Royal Court); *Anna Karenina* (Royal Exchange); *Our Ladies of Perpetual Succour, Glasgow Girls, In Time O' Strife, My Shrinking Life, Enquirer, An Appointment with the Wicker Man, Knives in Hens, Girl X, Mary Queen of Scots Got Her Head Chopped Off, Our Teacher's a Troll, Venus as a Boy* (National Theatre of Scotland); *Debuts* (National Theatre of Scotland/ Traverse); *Woyzeck, A Streetcar Named Desire, Show 3, Glitterland, A Series of Impossible Tasks, Show 6, Stab in the Dark* (Secret Theatre, Lyric Hammersmith); *Any Given Day, While You Lie, The Dark Things* (Traverse); *Pangaa* (Ankur Productions); *Huxley's Lab, Spring Awakening* (Grid Iron/Lung Ha's); *Caged, Pobby and Dingan, The Book of Beasts* (Catherine Wheels); *Under Milk Wood* (Theatre Royal, Northampton); *The Wasp Factory* (Cumbernauld Theatre); *The Wall* (Tron); *Great Expectations* (Byre Theatre/Prime Productions); *Travels with My Aunt* (New Wolsey).

TOM GIBBONS
Sound Designer & Composer
Tom's credits include: *People, Places and Things* (National Theatre/ West End); *The Crucible* (Broadway); *The White Devil, As You Like It* (RSC); *The Lorax* (Old Vic); *Translations* (ETT/Crucible); *A View from the Bridge* (Young Vic/West End/Broadway/Paris); *Happy Days, A Season in the Congo, Disco Pigs* (Young Vic); *Mr Burns* (Almeida); *Oresteia, 1984* (Almeida/West End); *The Absence of War, Romeo & Juliet* (Headlong); *Lion Boy* (Complicite); *Henry IV, Julius Caesar* (Donmar/St. Ann's Brooklyn); *Anna Karenina* (Royal Exchange); *Breeders* (St James), *Grounded* (Gate); *The Spire* (Salisbury Playhouse); *London, The Angry Brigade* (Paines Plough/Bush); *Roundabout Season* (Paines Plough/ Shoreditch Town Hall); *The Rover* (Hampton Court Palace); *Love Love*

Love (Paines Plough/Royal Court); *Island* (National Theatre, tour); *Dead Heavy Fantastic* (Liverpool Everyman); *The Moderate Soprano, Elephants* (Hampstead); *Plenty* (Crucible Studio); *Wasted* (Paines Plough, tour); *Chalet Lines, The Knowledge, Little Platoons, 50 Ways to Leave Your Lover* (Bush); *The Hairy Ape, Shivered, Faith, Hope and Charity, The Hostage, Toad* (Southwark Playhouse); *Sold* (Theatre503); *The Chairs* (Ustinov); *The Country, The Road to Mecca, The Roman Bath, 1936, The Shawl* (Arcola); *Utopia, Bagpuss, Everything Must Go, Soho Streets* (Soho); *Hitchcock Blonde* (Hull Truck).

CAROLINA VALDÉS
Movement Director
Carolina is Co-Artistic Director of Theatre O. She trained at the École Internationale de Théâtre Jacques Lecoq in Paris and at the Col·legi de Teatre in Barcelona.

Movement direction includes: *Treasure Island* (National Theatre, as Creative Associate); *Hamlet* (RSC); *Julius Caesar* (as Associate); *Absurdia* (Donmar); *Napoli Millionaria* (Central School of Speech and Drama); *The Resistible Rise of Arturo Ui* (Liverpool Playhouse).

Acting includes: *Henry IV* (Donmar); *The Late Henry Moss* (Southwark Playhouse); *The Secret Agent, Delirium* (Barbican/Abbey, Dublin), *Astronaut* (Barbican), *The Argument, 3 Dark Tales* (Barbican/international tour), and *Bond* (all for Theatre O); *Julius Caesar* (Donmar), *The Thirteen Midnight Challenges of Angelus Diablo* (RSC), *Casanova* (Told by an Idiot at Lyric Hammersmith); *Lindy's Got a Gun* (Trafalgar Studios); *The Barber of Seville, Carmen* (Opera 21).

Film and TV includes: *At the Threshold* (Daria Martin); *A Little Chaos* (Alan Rickman), *Call the Midwife* (BBC). Directing includes: *Reykjavik* and *The Garden* (Shams); *All Mapped Out* (Gogolia); *The Barber of Seville, Carmen* (Opera 21).

HOLLY ROSE HENSHAW
Costume Supervisor
Holly trained at the Royal Central School of Speech and Drama.

Her recent theatre credits include: *Luce* (Southwark Playhouse); *Forget Me Not* (Bush); *The One that Got Away* (Ustinov Studio); *Dan & Phil: The Amazing Tour Is Not on Fire* (UK tour); *Handbagged* (UK tour); *French Without Tears, When We Were Women* (Orange Tree); *The Suicide* (Embassy); *Octagon, House of Mirrors and Hearts* (Arcola); *The Marriage of Figaro, Lucia Di Lammermoor* (Diva Opera European tour); *The Father* (Trafalgar Studios); *The Argument, The Meeting, A Further Education, Sunspots, Deluge, Deposit, The Wasp, Elephants* and *State Red* (Hampstead); *Donkey Heart* (Trafalgar Studios/Old Red Lion);

The Armour (Langham Hotel, London); *Goodnight Children Everywhere* (Drama Centre London); *Don Giovanni, The Tales of Hoffman* (Diva Opera, Eurpean Tour); *Beanfield* (Bike Shed); Olympic and Paralympic Opening and Closing Ceremonies (2012).

As Associate Costume Designer for Snapdragon Productions: *Toast* (UK tour/59E59, New York), *Teddy* (Southwark Playhouse), *Toast, The Dead Wait* and *Thark* (Park); *A Life* (Finborough).

Film and TV includes: *Mr Turner* (Milke Leigh), *True Stories* (BBC2).

CHARLOTTE BEVAN
Casting Consultant
Charlotte is Casting Associate at the National Theatre, where she has worked on over fifty productions since 2012. Recent work includes: *Les Blancs, Here We Go, Husbands & Sons, Our Country's Good, Light Shining in Buckinghamshire, Rules for Living*. Previously she was Head of Casting at Shakespeare's Globe 2008 – 2012. Other work includes *Barbarians* (Young Vic – JMK 2015 winner); *Wildefire* (Hampstead) *Twelfth Night/Richard III* (Apollo Theatre/Belasco Theatre, New York); *Shakespeare Uncovered* (BBC/Blakeway); *The Spire* (Salisbury Playhouse); *The Two Gentlemen of Verona, The Talented Mr Ripley* (Royal Theatre, Northampton); *Telling Tales* (Print Room).

The Brink

For Al Smith

Characters

Nick, *twenty-eight – a secondary school teacher*
Chloe, *twenty-eight – a project manager*
Jo, *thirty-four – a secondary school teacher*
Mr Boyd, *forty-three – head teacher at the school*
Martin, *thirty-six – Chloe's boss*
Jessica, *fifteen – a student*
One, Two, Three, *fifteen – students*

Doubling can occur where necessary, played ideally with a company or four as follows –

Nick
Chloe/Jessica/student two
Jo/student three
Mr Boyd/Martin/student one

Setting and sound
Transient, non-naturalistic. Uniform and efficient like a textbook.

Note on the text
. . . denotes speech trailing off

/ denotes interruption

Part One

One

The present. Night time.

Nick *is alone on the school field.*

Nick   So it starts like any other day. I get up and I shower
and just like any other day I quit my job. Luckily for me I've
never had the courage of my convictions, so by the time I
brush my teeth I've already talked myself down from the
ledge. If I quit teaching I have no idea where I'd end up –
dead, or you know, worse. I never remember the journey to
work, and it's weird because after the shower I'm just there
bang outside the school. And there's fire everywhere. Half
the building's torn to shit. There's nothing left of the Maths
block. It's just fire and cinder and I'm stood there, stood
there watching this yawning hell and I say *what's happened*
and someone says *a bomb's gone off*. And I say *where's a bomb
come from* and they say *the Brink*. But I don't know what that
means. See I've never even heard of the Brink. And so I just
say again, *where the fuck's a bomb come from?*

Two

Earlier.

It's dark. **Chloe** *turns the light on. The kitchen.*

Nick *is sat eating cereal.*

Chloe   'kin hell.

Nick   Sorry.

Chloe   Sat in the dark. Scared me to shit.

Nick   Yeah, sorry.

Chloe   What are you doing?

Nick   Having breakfast.

Chloe   It's half five. Why've you got the light off?

Nick   Couldn't sleep. You going for your run?

Chloe   Yeah.

She sits.

Maybe.

Beat.

No.

Nick   No?

Chloe   I don't think I can do it anymore.

Nick   Only started yesterday.

Chloe   I just don't think it's me. Day two and I'm already in tears putting my trainers on. Who runs on purpose, for fuck sake? It's perverse.

Nick   If you don't enjoy it then don't do it.

Chloe   It's not that simple though, is it, Nick? Can't mess around anymore. We're in our late twenties and late twenties might as well be early thirties and early thirties might as well be forties and forties might as well be fifty. We're nearly fucking *fifty*, Nick. We've got to look after ourselves.

Nick   Christ. Right. What are you going to do then?

Chloe   You can sweat yourself fit. Read about it the other day. I might do that. Don't have to get up early to sweat, do you? Do you want a cup of tea?

Nick   Yeah go on.

She goes to make tea.

Chloe   Was I snoring?

Nick   What?

Chloe Are you up because I was snoring?

Nick No, you weren't snoring, no.

Beat.

Do you understand your dreams? Like, what they're about.

Chloe Why? What do I say?

Nick Nothing.

Chloe Pretty unfair if you're criticising me for something I say in my sleep.

Nick No, you don't say anything. I'm just asking whether or not you understand what your dreams mean.

Chloe Oh. Well, no. But who does?

Nick So they're just nonsense?

Chloe You can't worry about stupid sex dreams, Nick.

Nick Sex dreams? Where did you get sex dreams from?

Chloe That's what you mean, isn't it? About who you have sex with in your dreams?

Nick No.

Chloe Oh.

Nick You dream about us having sex?

Chloe Well . . .

Nick Who are you having sex with in your dreams, Chloe? Fucking hell.

Chloe I don't know.

Nick How can you not know?

Chloe I don't know. I can't see their faces.

Nick Why can't you see their face? Because it's from behind?

Chloe What?

Nick Do you mean you can't see their face because they're having sex with you from behind?

Chloe Nick, I don't /

Nick / Did you say *face* or *faces*?

Chloe Why does it matter?

Nick I'm just interested. How often do you . . . you know.

Chloe How often do I what? How often do I come?

Nick No. How often do you dream, holy shit, you can come more than once?

Chloe Why are you even asking me? What's this about?

Nick I don't know, I just . . . I just had this dream about the school. About something really bad happening at the school.

Chloe A sex dream at the school?

Nick No. Not a . . . But it was horrible, Chloe. Really dark.

Chloe Christ. You're properly freaked out.

Nick A bit. I mean, it wouldn't mean anything though would it?

Chloe I suppose if it's a one-off . . .

Nick I've had it a few times.

Chloe Right.

Nick It's quite a violent dream. There's a lot of blood. But it can't mean anything. Can it?

Chloe What are you actually doing in the dream?

Nick No, I'm not doing anything. It's not me.

Chloe Oh good.

Nick I'm not like . . .

Chloe   No, that's a relief.

Nick   Jesus.

Chloe   I know. That's what I thought.

Nick   But the sight of it, in my imagination, is enough to wake me up. It's enough to get me out of bed and want to sit in the dark on my own. That's quite intense that, isn't it?

Chloe   Do you think you might be depressed?

Nick   Depressed? Why would you say that?

Chloe   It's a sign, isn't it, not being able to sleep.

Nick   Having bad dreams? Everyone has bad dreams.

Chloe   The dream's just detail.

Nick   I really don't think I'm depressed.

Chloe   What if we decorated?

Nick   *Decorated*? Where did that come from?

Chloe   I read this thing about stasis. Stasis is like the environment where depression and lethargy and, and a lack of enthusiasm fester. It's a psychological thing. Change is the first step towards fighting it.

Nick   Where the hell did you read that?

Chloe   Online.

Nick   We're not in stasis.

Chloe   We haven't decorated since we moved in.

Nick   That's not true. I put up those Batman posters and then you took them down. That's like *two* redecorations.

Chloe   We moved in after university. It's like we're still living in a student house and it's nothing to be proud of, Nick. At our age, it's really not. We should be more like Yani and Tim. They bought a house and they're not depressed.

Nick   Buying houses . . . We're not Tories, Chloe.

Chloe   You can't just call anyone who shows any ambition in life a Tory.

Nick   You used to.

Chloe   I'm starting to look back and maybe the really hard-working kids at uni weren't the dickheads we said they were. Maybe they were just smart. I don't know how much we've got to show for where we are in our lives.

Nick   You're getting all this from one article?

Chloe   No, Nick. Loads of articles. It's what normal people talk about. Moving, decorating . . .

Nick   Going running at five in the morning?

Chloe   Yes, exercise as well.

Nick   Look, you can't let all that kind of nonsense get into your head. It's noise, is all it is. You work with a lot of people who are older than you. That can have an effect on your brain. You start to think like them.

Chloe   Like you working with kids, you mean?

Nick   That's different. I don't listen to the kids. Besides, they hate me.

Chloe   They don't hate you. What about Year 8 and the card they got you on your birthday?

Nick   No one likes Year 8. Do you know how embarrassing that was? In front of Year 9 as well. Now that's a year to impress.

Chloe   Nick, I'm worried that we're not normal. I'm worried that we should have moved on from here. And maybe you're worried too. Maybe that's why you're depressed.

Nick   I'm not depressed.

Chloe But you're up at half five eating cereal in the dark. So there's something. Isn't there?

Three

Later that morning.

The staffroom.

Jo Here, look at this.

Nick What is it?

Jo Marking from last night. A key lesson for you, Nick. What does it look like?

Nick Looks like he's got it all wrong.

Jo Exactly. But see, he does pretty solid in class. Why do you reckon his homework's shit?

Nick I don't know. Spends no time on it? Rushes it in the morning?

Jo No. The opposite. He's sat at that kitchen table for hours. Look at his handwriting. Better than in class. You know why his handwriting's so good but the work's so crap?

Nick I give up.

Jo Parents. Cheating fucking parents.

Nick Really?

Jo You can tell when the parents have had a crack at helping. They're always worse than the kids.

Nick How does that work?

Jo Well think about it. Your kid's here day after day learning real bloody technical stuff, maybe you might want to step away from the coursework when all you do is dick around on Facebook all day.

Nick   Right, yeah. That's good to know. To keep an eye out for.

Jo   Don't blame the kid. Never blame the kid. It's the arrogance of adults.

Nick   Arrogance of adults, I like that.

Jo   Course, you can't say anything. Parents are sacred. If it wasn't for the parents then we wouldn't have a job. And don't they know it. Had one the other day ask me if I could recommend somewhere they could take their kids on the weekend. I said yeah, *home*. Like, parent them yourselves for two days a week.

Nick   I can't believe the adult got all these fucking answers wrong.

Jo   Mrs Richardson just heard you say *fucking*.

Nick   Ah really? I get funny about old people hearing me swear. Like I'm letting them down.

Jo   How's it letting them down?

Nick   It's like they've given me this language and all I'm doing is using it to say fuck.

Jo   You don't think they said fuck?

Nick   Yeah but they said it like *fuck the Nazis, fuck . . . polio*. What are we saying fuck to? Wifi?

Jo   I'm sure she hears worse. She's got Year 10 biology.

Nick   Year 10 are savages. I don't know what it is about them. Maybe she can block it out. Like she has a filter. I don't have a filter. I soak it up like a sponge. No wonder Chloe thinks I'm depressed.

Jo   You're not depressed. You're stressed.

Nick   You think?

Jo   Textbook, mate.

Nick Oh phew, I thought there was something . . . you know, serious.

Jo Stress is serious. It could kill you, Nick.

Nick Stress could kill me? Like on its own or with something else?

Jo On its own.

Nick Well that's pretty stressful. You think I'm more stressed than normal?

Jo I don't know. You tell me.

Nick I'm not sleeping well but that's it. I keep getting this dream where . . . Well, whatever. It's just a dream.

Jo Just a dream? Never *just* a dream, Nick.

Nick What do you mean?

Jo Dreams are important. Dreams are signals.

Nick Signals?

Jo They're your subconscious trying to tell you something.

Nick You really believe that?

Jo It's serious stuff. Your subconscious is the point your body and your head connect. You're just at one end of the line. What happens in the dream?

Nick I don't know if I want to say.

Jo It's a sex dream?

Nick No. What's everyone . . . No, it's . . . Look, it doesn't matter what it's about. If my mind's trying to tell me something then why doesn't it say? It says when I need to sit down or eat or something.

Jo This isn't like needing to eat. I'm talking about deep psychological things.

Nick   I don't know if I want to listen to deep psychological things.

Jo   Ignore it if you want, but that's a risk you're deciding to take.

Nick   Oh no. It'd be a risk to . . . you know. I don't take risks. I like to play it safe.

Jo   But you're taking a risk thinking you know what safe is. Safe isn't always an option.

Nick   You think?

Jo   Think of a cat in the middle of a busy road. There's no safe way of getting to either side with all these cars like zooming past in both directions. The cat's got to be aware of the risks. But it's also got to move, it's got to get through the traffic to, to /

Nick   / But what if the cat just stays there, waiting for all the traffic to pass?

Jo   A cat sat in the road is taking a bigger risk than a cat running across it. Think about it.

Nick   I don't know. Life can't be that intense, even for cats.

Jo   Well it's what happened this morning and I went bang right over it.

Nick   Over what?

Jo   The cat.

Nick   This actually happened? I thought it was just a metaphor. Holy shit. Poor cat.

Jo   Poor cat? It made its choices.

Nick   What did you do?

Jo   What do you mean?

Nick   You didn't stop?

Jo   Where could I stop? I was on my way to the school.

Nick   How old was it?

Jo   It was definitely an older cat. Adult to mature.

Nick   Oh. Well that's something. I mean, don't get me wrong – kill nothing. But it's a cat that's lived its life.

Beat.

Nightingale still isn't in. That means I've got her lunch club then.

Jo   Didn't you hear? It's cancer.

Nick   Cancer . . . What can you do with cancer?

Jo   You can hope.

Nick   That's true.

Jo   But she is dying.

Nick   Well. It is cancer.

Jo   There's a card going round.

Nick   Well, yeah.

Jo   Yeah, but /

Nick   / I should sign it.

Jo   Course you should sign it. But see the /

Nick   / I really need to make sure. You can't not sign these things.

Jo   You're going to sign it, Nick. Will you let me finish? What I was saying is that this card has got Jesus on it.

Nick   Jesus Christ?

Jo   What other Jesus is there? It's not like saying Paul. Paul who? Paul McKenna? Paul McCartney? Jesus is Jesus. Like Prince.

Nick   Is Prince his name or is it his title?

Jo   It's a name. Where's he going to be prince of?
Minnesota?

Nick   Why Minnesota?

Jo   It's where he's from.

Nick   How do you know that?

Jo   I like Purple Rain. Will you let me tell you about this
fucking card?

Nick   Ok.

Jo   Well it's all *with sympathy* and that, like she's already
dead, and there on the front it's got Jesus on it. And I'm like
look isn't this a bit tasteless?

Nick   Why would it be tasteless? Is she Jewish?

Jo   No, she's not Jewish. I don't know what she is. But she's
not going to appreciate Jesus on a card.

Nick   Why not?

Jo   Because it's cancer, Nick. And a card like that is a sign.
It's a sign that if you believe in Jesus then you must also
believe in a reason for her cancer.

Nick   So you're saying because there's Jesus on the front it's
implying that God gave Mrs Nightingale cancer on purpose?

Jo   Exactly.

Nick   And what did they say?

Jo   They asked me if I wanted to get my own card.

Nick   And are you?

Jo   Course not. I wasn't telling you because I want to do
anything about it. Plus, Jesus came back. She won't. He's the
last person you want on a card.

Nick Mrs Nightingale . . . You never think it's going to be you, do you?

Jo It's what life does to you. You think you've got it all making sense and then . . . *boom*.

Nick Boom?

Jo Boom.

Four

That lunchtime.

Mrs Nightingale's class.

Jessica *enters.*

Nick Oh hey, yeah. Come in. I'm covering today.

Beat.

Does it normally start late?

Jessica No.

Nick Oh.

Beat.

What's your name?

Jessica Jessica Havens.

Nick I don't recognise you. What form are you in?

Jessica 10D.

Nick Oh Mr Davies.

Jessica Yeah.

Nick Sorry. I'm still learning names. I'm new. Well, last term. End of the term before last. That's not new at all, really, is it?

Beat.

We'll give it five minutes. Just waiting for the others.

Jessica   It's just me.

Nick   What?

Jessica   It's just me. That comes.

Nick   Why's it only you?

Jessica   I don't know. It's only ever me that does maths club.

Nick   Since when?

Jessica   Dunno.

Nick   How long's *dunno*? Weeks? Months?

Jessica   Months.

Nick   Months?

Jessica   Yeah.

Nick   Mrs Nightingale just does this for you? Every day? For months?

Jessica   Yeah.

Nick   Why?

Jessica   To get better at maths.

Nick   But it's lunchtime.

Jessica   I know.

Nick   No one else cares about getting better at maths at lunchtime. Are you bad at maths?

Jessica   No.

Nick   Then why are you here?

Jessica   I enjoy it.

Beat.

Nick   Good. That's good.

Jessica   Is Mrs Nightingale coming back?

Nick   No. I don't know. Yes. I hope so. Didn't you hear? She's got . . . ill. She's ill.

Jessica Oh.

Nick Yeah.

Jessica Should I go?

Nick What?

Jessica Should I go? If there's no maths?

Nick Well what would you do? About your . . .

Jessica I don't know.

Nick They'd be no maths club.

Jessica Yeah.

Nick I mean I don't want to just leave you. I suppose I can speak to Mr Boyd. Maybe someone else can keep it a regular thing.

Jessica Ok.

Nick But there's no reason why I can't do today. For the next week even. If they need me to. Until someone else can do it.

Jessica Thank you.

Nick What?

Jessica Nothing. I just said thank you.

Nick Oh. You're welcome.

Five

That afternoon.

In class.

Nick Mrs Nichols is off today so . . . Now that's not . . . Hey, can we quieten down? Now that's not licence to do nothing, ok? Has anybody not brought their textbooks?

Natalie, this is like the third lesson I've had you in this week and you've never had the right books. What's going on? Do you not have a timetable?

Peter, can you sit down, please? Why are you so excited?

Karen, stop chewing that.

Peter, Karen can stop chewing it on her own, thank you.

Everyone quieten down. I'm not sure where you've got with this so let's start at the beginning. Don't moan, this is revision. Ok so, *Tale of Two Cities*. Who wants to read?

No one. Ok. I'll read.

It was the best of times, it was the worst of times. It was the age of wisdom, it was the age of foolishness. It was the epoch of belief, it was the epoch of incredulity. It was the season of Light, it was the season of Darkness. It was the spring of hope, it was the winter of despair. We had everything before us, we had nothing before us.

Um, before we carry on. Can anyone tell me what this means?

It conveys the novel's central tensions, the themes. We have love and family on the one side and we have war and hatred and violence on the other. Dickens uses an anaphora . . . Can anyone tell me what an anaphora is?

Ok, so write this down. An anaphora is the repetition of a phrase at the beginning of consecutive clauses. *It was the age . . . it was the age, it was the epoch . . . it was the epoch . . .* Etcetera.

Dickens is suggesting that good and evil and light and dark stand equally matched. They're opposites, but they're connected, yeah? As ideas. Think of it like a road that goes North, it also goes South. The road itself points in both directions. It's all about which way you're facing. Can anyone think of any examples of their own?

What's that, Tim?

Awake and dreaming. Um, but I mean would, would you say that they are . . . Dreams are just . . . They're not part of the same thing. They're not connected. Are they? *Are they?*

Beat.

Hey so anyway, you all get the point. Let's move on to the . . . the next bit. Uh . . . How about you just read by yourselves in your heads? Ok?

In your head, Peter.

Six

Later that afternoon.

Mr Boyd's *office.*

Nick   But I know nothing of physics.

Mr Boyd   You know what it means to sit down. You know light and dark. These are fundamental physical things.

Nick   There's more to it than that.

Mr Boyd   But you can't say you know nothing. You're resourceful.

Nick   I'm completely lost with the sciences.

Mr Boyd   That's ok. No one's an expert.

Nick   But we're teachers. I think we're meant to be experts.

Mr Boyd   We have books and computers /

Nick   / If I'm covering for Mrs Patel then /

Mr Boyd   / and videos.

Nick   Then the students are going to know more than I do.

Mr Boyd   They'll be able to help you.

Nick   Help me teach them? How would that work? I don't know if I can teach a lesson I know nothing about.

Mr Boyd   You cover for maths. You cover for English.

Nick   And that's exactly what I wanted to talk to you about. I feel like I'm drowning in other people's classes. I haven't had a day of just my own classes in months.

Mr Boyd   History will still be there. Don't you worry about that. We're going through a very awkward period right now, Nick. A tragic and awkward . . . *tragically* awkward period. Mrs Nightingale /

Nick   / No, I know. I'm not trying to say /

Mr Boyd   / Mrs Nightingale has *cancer*.

Nick   I know she does. No, I know. I'm sorry. I don't mean to be . . . I suppose I'm just a little anxious at the moment, Mr Boyd. Does that make sense? I'm stressed.

Mr Boyd   Oh you're not stressed.

Nick   I'm not? Do you think I'm depressed?

Mr Boyd   No, you're not depressed either.

Nick   Then what's wrong with me?

Mr Boyd   You're modern. You're a very modern man, Nick.

Nick   Thank you . . .?

Mr Boyd   And it's no good for you. You never have a break from it. Constant noise. Look at your phone there. Buzzing away.

Nick   My phone's off.

Mr Boyd   And so suspicious. You never trust a thing anyone says.

Nick   I don't think that's true.

Mr Boyd   Now don't get me wrong, you've got to be worried. Don't be ignorant – there's so much to worry about. Violence. Catastrophe. I'm talking about the world. Not just your own life.

Nick No, well, that's what I thought.

Mr Boyd A little anxiety is good for you. It shows you're paying attention. Keeps you on your toes.

Nick But too much of it can kill you.

Mr Boyd I don't think that's right. I've never heard of anyone dying of worry. Now you've only been here a few months. You'll settle in.

Nick I think there's more to it than just settling in, Mr Boyd.

Mr Boyd Teaching brings with it a unique set of challenges.

Nick I know.

Mr Boyd It can be a lot to deal with. Not everybody can teach. You've got here and that's a lot more than most.

Nick I think my, my anxiety is manifesting itself in my thoughts. Pictures. And it makes me worry about my job. I know that how I feel about myself must be having some effect on the pupils. Like they can smell my doubt or something.

Mr Boyd Children don't know what they can smell.

Nick Maybe it's that I don't know where I should be heading.

Mr Boyd How old are you?

Nick I'm twenty-eight.

Mr Boyd Well.

Nick Well what?

Mr Boyd Well that's where you're going wrong. You're twenty-eight. You've probably got to where you're going. You don't feel like you're getting anywhere because you're already there.

Nick But that's not comforting at all. I don't think I could live with myself if I died without achieving more.

Mr Boyd So is that it, Nick? You're scared of dying?

Nick Of course I am. Who isn't? Mr Boyd, I'm not sleeping very well.

Mr Boyd Oh.

Nick *Oh*? Why *oh*?

Mr Boyd You said you were stressed but you didn't mention sleep. Sleep's important. Don't you know you need to sleep?

Nick It's not . . . I mean, yes of course I do. It's not out of choice.

Mr Boyd Sleep is vital for a healthy brain.

Nick I've been starting to have very strange dreams.

Mr Boyd All dreams are strange, Nick. They're meant to be strange. Very strange.

Nick Not like these dreams.

Mr Boyd What happens in them?

Nick I don't know if I want to /

Mr Boyd / Yes I remember my first years in the teaching game. Geography, it was. I was torn to bits day after day. You'll soon get used to it. That mild panic. You get tuned out of it. It'll hum like a fridge and you don't hear the hum of fridges, do you?

Nick I don't know if I can do that. Mr Boyd, I /

Mr Boyd / Yes you can, Nick. Yes you can.

Nick Mr Boyd, I dream about a bomb under the school. I dream that there's this bomb and every night it explodes. I don't want it in my head and I can't ignore it like you say I should.

Beat.

It probably means nothing, though. It means nothing, right? It's just like a . . . I mean, you know what it's like. Imaginations. Strange dreams. You know?

Beat.

Mr Boyd?

Mr Boyd Funny.

Nick What's funny? How's that funny?

Mr Boyd Yes, very clever. Very sharp.

Nick I don't understand.

Mr Boyd *I've been having dreams. The bomb, the bomb.* Yes, fair play. I didn't see it coming at all. You pranked me. One nil.

Nick Mr Boyd, it isn't a prank. I'm being serious.

Mr Boyd It's a funny joke, Nick. But don't milk it.

Nick I'm not milking anything. I don't know what you're talking about.

Mr Boyd You're teasing me about the bomb. The old one up on the Brink.

Nick I was talking about my dream, Mr Boyd. There's a bomb? Like an actual, real bomb? It was the Brink in my dream. They said it was the Brink. Why am I dreaming about a, a . . .?

Mr Boyd You didn't know?

Nick No!

Beat.

Mr Boyd I did wonder who would've approved of your knowing. You don't seem their type. And I appear to have just let the little bugger slip out, haven't I? Oh dear.

Nick   Are you really telling me there's a bomb up on the playing fields, Mr Boyd?

Mr Boyd   Oh it's all perfectly safe. It's an old deactivated World War Two bomb. Left from the Blitz. Couldn't move it. Too big, it was. Covered in concrete now. You'll have to promise me to keep it to yourself. This gets out and people would overreact.

Nick   They'd overreact? Mr Boyd, this is madness. A bomb at the school and you're keeping it a secret? Why would someone build a school on top of a bomb?

Mr Boyd   Well, they didn't. The fields were never meant to be part of the school.

Nick   Doesn't it seem bizarre to you that this is exactly what I've been dreaming of? This exact thing? Except in my dream it explodes.

Mr Boyd   Now, Nick . . .

Nick   What if it's . . . a vision? What if my dreams are a sign that it'll explode?

Mr Boyd   It's been down there for so long. Who says it's going to explode?

Nick   Because it's meant to. That's its job.

Mr Boyd   I don't think we should get too excited.

Nick   Has anybody even checked it recently? I mean, if it's under concrete then we've got no idea what condition it's in. It could explode any second. I don't like the idea of not knowing, Mr Boyd. Don't you think we should do something about it?

Mr Boyd   You *are* doing something. You're making a rational decision not to alarm people.

Nick   All this, I mean, it's a lot to take in.

Mr Boyd But not impossible. You can take this in, Nick. Concentrate and it will go in.

Nick How can I teach on top of a bomb?

Mr Boyd You'll find a way. You'll have to. We need you at your best. Education is a fragile, dear vocation. You are the world to many children here. Their very lives are in your hands.

Seven

That afternoon.

The school fields.

Students *are running.*

Three Keep up, sir.

Two Come on, sir.

Nick I'm coming. Just keep going.

Three We don't know where to go, sir.

Nick Past the fence.

One Where?

Nick Past the . . .

He catches up with them.

I said past the fence. Let's have two minutes then. Catch our breath.

Two We don't need to catch our breath, sir.

One We want to keep going.

Nick No, no. Breaths are important. Don't you learn anything in biology? It's . . . I don't know. It's for your muscles or whatever.

Three We're meant to be running, sir.

Nick   We are running. We're just recapping on what we've run so far.

Two   We don't normally have to wait for the teacher.

Nick   Yeah well it's not my lesson.

Two   But you're an adult. Shouldn't be this out of puff, sir.

Three   Are you dying, sir?

Nick   Of course I'm not dying.

Three   Don't you worry though?

Nick   About what?

Three   Dying, sir.

Nick   I'm not . . . I'm not dying.

One   You were sweating putting your trainers on.

Nick   That doesn't mean I'm dying. That's just a problem with salt.

One   Must be a worry though, mustn't it? Not being able to run.

Nick   I can run if I want to.

Two   Is it scary being old, sir?

Nick   I don't know. What kind of question is that?

Two   Scares me.

Three   Yeah, scares me too.

Nick   I'm not as old as you think I am. How old do you think I am?

Two   Twenty-eight.

Nick   That's . . . Well, it's not that old, is it?

Three   Is Mrs Nightingale still alive, sir?

Nick   Yes, she's still alive. How'd you get from my age to Mrs Nightingale? Twenty-eight is still young. Not as young as you, granted.

Three   I was just wondering how she's doing, sir.

Nick   She's ok, I think. I don't know. It's cancer. You never know with cancer, do you? Look. Come on. Let's go back. We'll go back the way we came and, I don't know, round the cricket square. That's enough for the day.

Two   Oh but, sir, we've only just got to the Brink.

Nick   I thought that was the Brink over there. The ledge in the grass.

One   Brink curves round, sir.

Nick   We're on the Brink now? That's . . . It comes this far? This is a slant, not a brink . . . Why would you call . . .

Three   Are you alright, sir?

Nick   You wouldn't have any idea just by looking at it.

One   Look at what?

Nick   The ground.

Two   Sir?

Nick   Does it feel warm to you? It feels warm. On your hands. Burning under the surface. How can he say that it's safe?

Three   What's safe?

Nick   Exactly. What is safe? We don't know. Don't you feel it? Can't you feel it under your feet?

One   Feel what, sir?

Nick   Under the ground here, right directly under us is a . . . a . . .

Two   A what?

Beat.

Three   What are you talking about, sir?

Nick   Nothing. No, nothing. Let's . . . let's go back. Run back that way.

One   But, sir, we came from that way.

Nick   Yeah well think of it as revision. Look at the time. Don't want to be late for your next class. Come on. You lot run on, I'll catch you up.

The students run on.

Nick *has a moment on the Brink.*

He hears a sound.

Hello?

Mr Boyd (*off*)   It's me, Nick.

Nick   Mr Boyd. What . . .

Mr Boyd *walks up.*

Nick   What are you doing out on the . . .?

Mr Boyd   I saw you come up here. With your class.

Nick   I didn't realise the Brink came out this far. Did you follow us?

Mr Boyd   You wanted to tell them.

Nick   Of course I wanted to. Were you . . . were you making sure that I didn't?

Mr Boyd   No. Of course not. I didn't need to anyway. You thought better of it.

Nick   I couldn't do it. I couldn't find the words.

Mr Boyd   You felt a responsibility. A responsibility to calm.

Nick   It's more that I wouldn't know where to start.

Mr Boyd Even after you left my office I still wasn't sure whether or not you were joking with me. And I realised that you couldn't have been. You don't have an ounce of humour in your body, Nick. And that worried me. Of course, you're going to have to tell me who told you about the bomb.

Nick I'm being serious, Mr Boyd. I promise you that nobody told me. It was just these dreams. These dreams that I made up in my in my own head and they happen to be true. Can't you see how this is more worrying for me? I mean, I wonder if I need to see someone.

Mr Boyd No. Never. You can never do that, Nick. We have had to keep the tightest of lids on this. And we've done a very good job. And so now are you. You're now another hand holding up this great weight. You're part of something important. Could you imagine the chaos if it got out?

Nick But I thought you said it was safe.

Mr Boyd Let's not be naïve, Nick. It's not the bomb itself that I'm worried about. Enough damage can be done with the word alone. You say *bomb* and it paints a terrible picture. They're children. They have precious, tender minds and a head can break only once.

Nick But what about the parents? A carefully worded letter might /

Mr Boyd / The parents would be even worse. Parents expect schools to be a refuge from today, a vestige for their own nostalgia. School to your parent is where custard is still pink and dinner ladies are still obese in a fun way. These parents had no other way into the world and can't imagine any other way for their children. We tell them about the bomb today and this school will never be the same. And you don't want that, Nick. It would work out very poorly for you.

Nick Are you threatening me, Mr Boyd?

Mr Boyd No. Of course not. No. Not at all.

Nick   Oh that's a relief.

Mr Boyd   But I am talking about the delivery and provision of education for young people in the surrounding area. Which I know you care very much about.

Nick   Of course I do.

Mr Boyd   And so if something was to come out that would disrupt our students' progress . . . A rumour about a bomb, perhaps, after all this time keeping it a tip-top secret . . . Well, it wouldn't take an expert to work out whose fault that would be. And if that was to happen, well never mind what other people would think, we both know that you'd just have to kill yourself.

Nick   *Kill* myself? Did you say kill myself?

Mr Boyd   No, I said that we both know that you just wouldn't be able to live with yourself.

Nick   Right. Because I thought you said /

Mr Boyd   / I am trusting you here, and I know that you are trusting yourself, to do the right thing.

He starts walking away.

Nick   So what should I do about the dreams then, Mr Boyd?

Beat.

Mr Boyd?

Part Two

One

The present. Night time.

Nick *is on the school field.*

Nick So I'm stood there and the school starts to sag out of this blast hole like a punctured bladder. A punctured bladder on fire. I can't tell you how much fire there is. And I realise that the smell isn't coming from the brick or the softening glass, but from the bodies. And they're popping and crackling and going off in all sorts of colours like fireworks. And those that can't scream or cry are just making the others scream and cry even more. And I don't know what's worse – the dead or the dying. Some of them are shouting *Mum* and *Dad* but they're not really calling for their mums or dads at all – they're just begging the air. Then out of nowhere someone says *can you help me, sir?* And I can't. I know that I *can't.*

Two

Earlier.

The morning.

In the car.

Chloe Can you close your window?

Nick I like it open. I don't like the . . .

Chloe It stinks.

Nick What stinks? Who stinks?

Chloe Outside.

Nick   Outside? How can you say outside stinks? It's outside. There's so much of it. It can't all stink.

Chloe   There's a general smell. It must have been the park.

Nick   The park's the park. It's the city that stinks. Pollution and, and . . . The park is life. Kids playing up trees. Old men playing chess.

Chloe   Old men don't play chess in the park, Nick. Old men wank in the park.

Nick   Not in the daytime. At least not where you can see.

Beat.

No alarm clocks in the park. No one telling you what to do. No stress, no secrets. It's peace. It's paradise, Chloe.

Chloe   Are you drunk? Have you started drinking in the morning? Shit.

Nick   No. I'm not . . . I'm not drinking in the morning. I'm just . . . Hey, maybe I'm paying attention to the world for the first time in my life.

Pause.

Chloe   I was talking to Gina yesterday about your dreams and she /

Nick   / Hang on. Gina?

Chloe   And she said that bad dreams about the workplace often suggest anxiety about the future.

Nick   Why were you talking to Gina about my dreams?

Chloe   Because she knows.

Nick   What does she know?

Chloe   She studies what dreams mean. It's her thing. She's very good.

Nick Don't talk to Gina about my dreams, Chloe. Don't talk to anyone about my dreams. Bloody hell.

Chloe I was just asking for advice.

Nick Well, you shouldn't.

Chloe I can't do anything right.

Nick I don't want it getting out. I don't want people knowing about my dreams. Not before I've worked out what I should do about them.

Chloe You haven't even told me what happens in them so she couldn't /

Nick / Yeah well it's a good job I haven't otherwise it would've been broadcast all over the bloody BBC by now. And then I'd be in the shit.

Chloe Why would you be in the shit?

Beat.

Nick Telling Gina. I thought yoga was her thing, not dreams.

Chloe You can have more than one thing, Nick.

Nick *Bullshit* is her thing. It all comes under the umbrella of . . . bloody horseshit.

Chloe Well pick one. Horseshit and bullshit are two different things. The clues are in the names. Comes from different fucking animals.

Beat.

You can't just expect me to ignore it when you tell me you're having horrible dreams, Nick. You were petrified the other day. If you're going through something then you need to let me in. Or if not me then someone who can help you.

Nick Like who?

Chloe   There are people there . . . Specialists . . . Someone who can help you understand what it is.

Nick   Now, hang on.

Chloe   You shouldn't have to keep this a secret. You could even get a doctor to write a note to the school as well. Explaining what these dreams are and why you need more support. This is a big thing, Nick.

Beat.

Nick? Are you listening?

Nick   Yeah.

Chloe   There are people who would want to know.

Nick   No, I . . .

Chloe   Why don't I book you an appointment with the doctor at lunch?

Nick   They're . . . They've stopped.

Chloe   What?

Nick   They've stopped. The dreams have stopped.

Chloe   They've stopped?

Nick   Yeah. I don't know what it was. But they're gone.

Chloe   Just like that?

Nick   Just like that. So strange. Scary, you know. But they've stopped and I feel much better. In myself. I don't need to see a doctor.

Chloe   Why didn't you say?

Nick   I was embarrassed. I'm sorry.

Chloe   So you're not depressed?

Nick   No. Not any more than anyone else anyway. That's why I didn't want you talking to Gina. I didn't want you to panic. I'm sorry.

Pause.

Chloe   Since when?

Nick   Since when what?

Chloe   Since when did they stop?

Nick   I don't know. I slept pretty well last night.

Chloe   Last night could just be a one-off.

Nick   Bloody hell. Sounds like you want me to be having them, Chloe. Aren't you happy they've stopped? Isn't it good news?

Chloe   Yeah. No, of course.

Nick   I woke up this morning and I feel really, massively improved.

Chloe   Good.

Beat.

It just seems /

Nick   / What?

Chloe   It just seems a little quick. I mean, even if the dreams have stopped that doesn't mean that a sense of stasis isn't /

Nick   / You keep saying stasis. Stasis isn't a thing. And even if it was a thing then maybe it isn't a bad idea. Maybe I don't want change. Maybe I want everything to be fine and safe and just like it's meant to be. Nothing different, no surprises. You start uprooting and you don't know what you're going to uncover. Leave it be. Leave everything be.

Silence.

Chloe   It's Martin's tonight, remember.

Nick   Martin's what?

Chloe   We're going to Martin's. For dinner.

Nick   Oh shit. No. I forgot.

Chloe   Nick. You promised.

Nick   Ok. It's fine.

Chloe   *Fine*? Bloody hell, it's not asking for a lot is it?

Nick   I said it was fine. Fine is a good thing.

Chloe   Good is good. Fine is just fine.

Nick   Fine is accepting the fact of the event.

Chloe   I'm just asking you to sit and eat the food someone else has made you and be generally receptive to conversation. I mean, you spend all day trying to not tell kids to fuck off, maybe you can manage to be polite to my boss for a few hours, if you, like, really concentrate?

Nick   I'll try my best.

Chloe   It's nice he's invited us. This doesn't happen all the time you know. It's a sign that he's got plans and maybe I'm a part of them. Please, for my sake, behave.

Nick   I will.

Chloe   Thank you.

Beat.

Will you remember to wear a good shirt?

Nick   Isn't this a good shirt?

Chloe   No. Where am I parking?

Nick   Turn in here. In front of the buses. Fuck them.

Three

Later that morning.

The staffroom.

Jo . . . and so I get this feeling /

Nick / Jo.

Jo I'm stood there and I'm, like /

Nick / Jo, I'm a bit worried about /

Jo / No, let me finish. See it must've been /

Nick / No, I need to talk to you. Before the bell.

Jo After this. After. You need to hear it.

Nick But, Jo /

Jo / So it must've been the fish because it went through me like a fucking motorway. And so I'm there on the toilet. But the smell is so bad it's making me gag. And Thom's at the door, banging, and this is how I know it's the fish, because he needs to throw up too. So he's banging at the door and I'm like, *no you can't come in and see me shitting like this* because we might've got to that biblical stage in our relationship but we're still definitely New Testament, not Old Testament. But this is an emergency and before he knocks the door down I unlatch it and in he comes. Thankfully it's had a different effect on him so he's needing to throw it all up. So while I'm sat on the toilet he's in the bath, vomiting down the plughole. But that's not all. The smell from me is making him throw up even more and what with watching him throw up, my gagging starts to turn into full on retching and I'm having to lean over the sink and throw up in there while the world falls out of my arse. Watching me throw up is making him throw up more too so the pair of us are there throwing our guts up and you can imagine the mess. The bathroom starts off looking like a Pollock painting but ends up looking more like a Rothko.

Beat.

Oh and then he starts shitting too.

Beat.

What did you want to talk about?

Nick   I . . . I need your help with something, Jo. Something serious that I'm not even meant to talk about. You see /

She notices something.

Jo   / What the fuck is this?

Nick   What?

Jo   The rota. Why the fuck am I down doing your second period? And *why* am I covering your whole afternoon? Fucking hell, Nick.

Nick   What? Let me see.

Jo   I was trying to keep that free. You know how much marking I've got to do.

Nick   I'm not on the rota at all. I've been unrotaed.

Jo   I'm going to have to do my marking at home now. I'm going to have to work late and that's another night Thom and I can't have sex. Are you trying to ruin my life?

Nick   Jo, this is it. This is what I wanted to talk to you about. I know too much.

Jo   What?

Nick   Mr Boyd thinks I'm going to tell the pupils. He's keeping me out of the class so I can't tell anyone.

Jo   Tell anyone what? I've got no idea what you're going on about.

Nick   It's a secret that he's keeping from us, from the pupils. The school isn't safe. Mr Boyd told me himself. He admitted it. Right underneath the ground there's a . . . Why are you smirking? Jo, this isn't funny.

Jo I wouldn't listen to Boyd.

Nick Why not?

Jo He's been all over the place since Ashbury High closed.

Nick Ashbury High – the, the asbestos school?

Jo Yeah and Boyd's doing everything he can to get this place closed down too. He had Daniels chasing the birds on the roof because he was sure they were carrying impetigo.

Nick Why would Boyd want the school closed down?

Jo Think about it. They tear down these old schools and filter the kids off into bigger academies. The kind of academies that Boyd wants to work in. He's seeing all these heads with super-budgets and Apple computers and shit and look at us, we have to photocopy pages out of textbooks. He can't wait to get out. Except of course he can't quit because it would look bad on his CV. However, if the school happened to close . . .

Nick Then he can move on with his reputation intact.

Jo Even better, he'll look like the hero that saved all these kids from an unsafe school. Clever, no? So just ignore whatever he's told you. At some point he's going to have to prove it and when he can't, he'll just end up looking like even more of an idiot.

Nick It can't be that simple.

Jo It is.

Nick But there's a bomb, Jo. There's an actual bomb. Under the school. Left from the Second World War underneath the playing fields.

Beat.

Jo So that's how he'll do it.

Nick Do what?

Jo   They'd have to excavate the whole area. That kind of work would be too expensive. Easier to shut the whole place down.

Nick   But, Jo, he didn't tell me that the bomb was there. I found out and he admitted it because he thought I already knew.

Jo   Who told you then?

Nick   No one. See, it all matches perfectly with these dreams I've been having, where every night a bomb goes off and kills everyone.

Jo   And so you told Boyd you were having these dreams and he just said *well yeah funny you should say that.*

Nick   Kind of. Yeah.

Jo   Jesus.

Beat.

How do I know Boyd isn't just using you to spook up more teachers? Get them behind this bomb idea and then *make* him close the school?

Nick   Because he told me to keep it a secret. He threatened me.

Jo   He threatened you?

Nick   Well, he didn't quite threaten me but there was definitely an element of displeasure in, in the idea of me spreading the information. I'm only telling you because I'm going to fucking burst and I know you'd know what to do about it. I didn't even tell Chloe. I told her the dreams have stopped. I lied to her. I never lie to Chloe. Except maybe about how many carbohydrates I eat at lunch.

Jo   It doesn't make any sense.

Nick   None of it makes any sense and, and stuff like this, stuff like taking me off the rota, is only making me even more sure that this is some serious shit. I mean, if Boyd really is trying to get the school closed down then why's he going to all this effort to silence me?

Jo   Maybe he's waiting for a particular job. He's got his eye on something really specific, and you've found out too soon.

Nick   I don't know if I buy that, Jo.

Jo   You know it's the pupils I worry about. I don't know what game Boyd is playing but I don't trust it. I can't help you with this, Nick. Whatever you've got going on with Boyd. I don't want any part of it. I've got to be here for kids.

Nick   You were right about what you said about risks. Sometimes safe isn't an option.

Jo   What do you mean?

Nick   If I tell people then I'll end up in all sorts of trouble and the school will get closed down. But if I don't and the bomb goes off . . . then that's all my fault too because I didn't warn anybody. I'm that fucking cat in the middle of the road and cars are flying passed me and I can't stand still.

The bell goes.

Jo   Hey, if you're not around at break I'll presume you've been all chopped up and put in the pies at lunch.

Nick   Yeah or stuffed into the fucking walls. Who do you reckon's doing the maths club? It's not on the rota.

Jo   Nightingale's maths club? I seem to be doing everything else for you today, do you want me to cover it?

Nick   No. It's fine. I want to do it.

Four

Later that morning.

The basement.

Nick *is sat behind piles and piles of registers.*

Mr Boyd *enters*.

Mr Boyd   Knock knock.

Nick   Mr Boyd.

Mr Boyd   Look alive.

Nick   Yes, trying to.

Mr Boyd   Chilly down here. You could chill in this.

Nick   I wondered if I could have a heater down here?
There's one in the History storeroom. I wouldn't want to
catch a cold.

Mr Boyd   Oh you can't catch a cold indoors.

Nick   Can't you? I don't know if that's true.

Mr Boyd   How are you doing down here, Nick?

Nick   I'm making my way through it all. You get into quite
a rhythm. Date, sticker, folder, box. It's very straightforward.

Mr Boyd   Sorry to give you such an uninspiring task.
Someone every year draws the short straw for archiving
the registers.

Nick   I didn't realise there were straws to be drawn.

Mr Boyd   An important and vital . . . a vitally important
task. Now I don't want to disturb you any longer, I just
wanted to make sure you're still compos mentis. No windows
down here and that can send you a little loopy.

Nick   Well, if I could have that heater that I mentioned?

Mr Boyd   I definitely promise to look into it.

Nick   Thank you, Mr Boyd.

Mr Boyd *goes to leave*.

Nick   Mr Boyd, can I ask you a question?

Mr Boyd   Of course.

Nick   Now this might sound a little, uh, silly. But you don't have me down here because you're worried I'm going tell people about the bomb . . . Do you?

Mr Boyd   Is that what you think, Nick?

Nick   Well it just seems a bit of a coincidence to have me down here the day after I find out that there's a bomb under the school.

Mr Boyd   Rest assured. You being down here has nothing to do with yesterday.

Nick   Well that's a relief.

Mr Boyd   But when you say it like that it does sound a bit odd, doesn't it?

Nick   What?

Mr Boyd   No. Odd is the wrong word. In fact, it doesn't sound odd at all. As a matter of fact it sounds perfectly logical to, in my position, keep you away from the students. If that was my intention. Odd would be to accidentally leak to you some very sensitive information and then let you loose up there telling God knows who.

Nick   So . . . I'm confused. Mr Boyd, are you keeping me down here because of the bomb or not?

Mr Boyd   Life is quite confusing, isn't it, Nick?

Nick   Increasingly so, Mr Boyd.

Mr Boyd   Send up a call whenever you like and Mrs Jennings can make you a cup of tea.

Nick   Mr Boyd, I had another question.

Mr Boyd   Another one? Full of questions today, Nick.

Nick   It won't take long. I promise. It's just I had this textbook with me, for what we were going to work on in class today. You see, my Year 11s are doing World War Two at the moment.

Mr Boyd   Right.

Nick   And this book . . . It happens to be about the Battle of Britain. And, and the Blitz. And I've been reading it this morning . . .

Beat.

Mr Boyd, this part of town was never bombed in the Blitz, was it?

Mr Boyd   History was never my strong suit. I was a geography man myself.

Nick   It says it in here. They can be quite accurate about it. Because they recorded every single strike.

Mr Boyd   Yes.

Nick   So if the Germans never bombed this area, Mr Boyd, whose bomb is it under our school field?

Beat.

I was also reading a bit further on about how, after the war, instead of dismantling all of our own excess weapons and bombs, we, in times, buried them.

Mr Boyd   Did you really have time for all this reading this morning, Nick? These registers won't do themselves!

Nick   Mr Boyd, before the school expanded, was the Brink owned by the government?

Mr Boyd   Well, you'd have to ask the council about that.

Nick   Should I ask the council about that?

Mr Boyd   No. No, don't do that. Christ. You really do like to pick at scabs, don't you? Pick, pick, pick. They should have called you *Picholas* not . . . not Nicholas. Shouldn't they? Hey?

Nick   Are you ok, Mr Boyd?

Mr Boyd   They really should have windows in here too. Gets hard to breathe without daylight, doesn't it?

Nick   We're underground. I suppose windows would be hard to put in. Can I get you some water?

Mr Boyd   I don't want any water, Nick.

Beat.

It's true. It's all true. The bomb. The Blitz. The government. Whatever.

Nick   There's going to be more than one bomb down there isn't there?

Mr Boyd   I imagine so, yes.

Nick   We were developing some pretty incredible weapons in that war, Mr Boyd. Some pretty nasty stuff. Who knows what's down there.

Mr Boyd   Well you seem to have some pretty colourful ideas, Nick.

Nick   Has anyone ever checked the, the . . . what could be coming up out of the ground? Like, radiating out from these bombs?

Mr Boyd   What on earth are you talking about?

Nick   I worry about whether it could be having an effect on the students. There's a lot of violence at the school. The look in some of their eyes . . . What's growing underneath them? If the public knew about this . . . Mr Boyd, are you wanting to get the school shut down? Is this all a plan to, to get a good position in an academy?

Mr Boyd   Is that what you think? Is that what you think this is all about?

Nick   I don't know.

Mr Boyd   That shines me in a terrible light, Nick.

Nick   I know. I'm sorry. I didn't mean it. But we have to do something, right? The school should. The, the council. The government should! Do we need to call the government?

Mr Boyd   Nick, you are touching on something far greater than yourself. Greater than any of us here. I must warn you, you are meddling. And I don't think a meddling history teacher would curry much favour with . . . with . . .

Nick   With who?

Mr Boyd   Forces, Nick. Forces so strong they could crush you into liquid.

Beat.

This is a story whereby the likes of us aren't even characters.

Nick   So what do we do?

Mr Boyd   What do we *do*? For Christ's sake, we do nothing. *Nothing*. We keep our mouths shut and our eyes closed.

Nick   I wonder if whatever is under us is causing my dreams. I wonder if it's even caused Mrs Nightingale's cancer. I don't know if I can do nothing, Mr Boyd.

Mr Boyd   Ok, Nick. Follow that thought through. What exactly do you intend to do? Really? I mean, I admire this new energy in you but really, what on earth can *you* do? You can't even finish the fucking registers.

Pause.

Would you like to join me for lunch?

Nick   Lunch? No. No, I . . . Thank you but I have plans. I have to be at . . . I'm going for a walk.

Mr Boyd *goes to leave.*

Mr Boyd   Nick, you have been exposed to more here than you could have ever imagined. Who knows what damage this information may have caused you. I must warn you. This may manifest itself into a headache.

Five

That lunchtime.

Mrs Nightingale's class.

Nick   And so the, the fraction needs to be converted, right? It asks for the answer as a decimal.

Jessica   Oh yeah.

Nick   So do you remember how we do that?

Jessica   I divide it?

Nick   Yeah that's right. You divide the top number from the bottom. Do you remember what we call them?

Jessica   No.

Nick   No, that's fine. They're called the, the . . . Hey you know what, it doesn't matter what they're called, you just need to know how to do it.

Jessica   Are you ok, sir?

Nick   Yeah. If you just convert the answers to the rest then let me know.

Pause.

Jessica   Why are the blinds closed, sir?

Nick   What? Oh . . . To, to keep the light out. If it's too bright you can't see.

Beat.

Jessica   You seem a bit distracted today, sir.

Nick   What?

Jessica   Nothing. Sorry. I'll . . .

Nick   No, it's ok to talk. This isn't like normal class. I just didn't hear what you said.

Jessica   I said that you seem a little distracted, sir.

Nick   Oh. Yeah. No, I'm fine.

Jessica   I don't mean it rudely, sir.

Nick   No. No, you know what, I haven't been sleeping very well. That's all.

Pause.

Jessica   Is that why you haven't been in school all day, sir?

Nick   I . . . I've been in school. I've just been archiving registers. You noticed I wasn't around?

Jessica   We were just told you were going to cover our English class.

Nick   Oh. Right. Yeah. No. No, not today. Change of plan.

Silence.

What would you do, Jessica, if, say, a friend told you something that, that was meant to be a secret. But you know other people deserve to know about it?

Jessica   What kind of secret, sir?

Nick   It doesn't really matter about the, the secret exactly. More the point. I mean, it's a secret for a reason. And they think they're protecting people by not . . . not saying.

Jessica   Why did they tell me what the secret was if people aren't meant to know?

Nick   Because maybe you had a hunch about it. Maybe you kind of already knew.

Jessica   A secret about this friend?

Nick   No, it's a secret about the world. That this friend knows.

Jessica   If I went to the friend about a hunch I had about a secret then maybe it's because I trusted this friend to know what to do about it.

Nick But what if you don't trust your friend's judgement?

Jessica Then why are we friends?

Nick Ok maybe you're not friends. You just know each other. Look, I don't mean to . . . This is getting more complicated than I intended. I, uh . . . It doesn't matter.

Pause.

Jessica What are the consequences of the secret? Will people get in trouble?

Nick Yeah. You could say that. People would get hurt.

Jessica Hurt?

Nick Possibly. Maybe. I don't know. There's the potential for it to hurt people.

Jessica Then you have to ignore your friend and tell someone.

Nick You think?

Jessica I mean, that's what I'd do.

Nick Ok, so what if another friend though also said to you that telling people would /

/ The bell goes.

Oh hey look. The time. Already. Sorry, look let's crack on with these next time. But you get the rule, yeah?

Jessica Yeah.

Nick That's all it is. You just find the rule and stick to it.

She goes to leave.

I don't mean to put pressure on you with . . . I don't mean to burden you with stuff you don't need to worry about.

Jessica I'm not a kid.

Nick   No, quite right. But this, it's not what we're meant to be talking about now. This is maths club, not, you know, Nick's anxiety club.

Jessica   We want our teachers to tell us the truth.

Nick   I don't know if I'm allowed to do that.

Jessica   But if you won't tell us the truth, then who will?

Six

That afternoon.

The corridor.

Jo *is with* **Nick**.

Jo   What are we doing, Nick? Everyone's gone home. I need to get off myself.

Nick   This won't take long.

Jo   But why are we stood in the corridor outside Boyd's /

Mr Boyd *enters.*

Nick   Mr Boyd.

Mr Boyd   Nick. Jo. How can I help you?

Nick   Mr Boyd. Can we have a quick word?

Jo   Nick?

Mr Boyd   In my office? I've already locked up.

Nick   Ok well out here will do.

Jo   Nick, what are you doing?

Nick   Mr Boyd, the recent revelations about the school have shocked me and, and haunted me. I think we need to tell people the truth about what's underneath the school fields. Because if we won't tell the truth then who will? We're teachers, for Christ's sake. It's what the students, it's what the public, deserve. And, and I know what you're going to say and yes it is very ominous and terrifying and I'm sure there will be consequences with the crushing and the liquid and what-have-you. But, I tell you this, whatever's going on, you can silence one teacher without a hassle but you can't silence two. Jo knows about the bombs. And we won't stand for anything less than a full inquiry and, and an assurance that whatever's under the ground here will be cleared.

Beat.

Mr Boyd Is this true, Jo? Are you with Nick in this?

Jo No.

Nick What?

Jo No. I don't know what he's talking about, Mr Boyd.

Nick Jo.

Jo I told you I don't want to be part of this, Nick. You didn't listen to me.

Nick But this is serious. You do know what I'm talking about. Tell him that you do.

Jo I don't want the school to close down.

Nick Jo. I thought you were my friend. I thought you had my back.

Jo I'm here for the kids. Someone has to be. And some rumour about a /

Nick / Rumour? You still don't believe me?

Jo No. I don't believe that there's a bomb under the school.

Nick But, Jo, the Germans didn't even bomb the . . . So you need proof? Is that what this is?

Mr Boyd Look, I'm sorry to have dragged you into this here, Jo. Had I have known . . . I don't mean to be wasting your time.

Nick I can't believe it. You, you're making me out to look insane.

Jo Is there anything else, Mr Boyd?

Mr Boyd No. I'll see you tomorrow.

Jo goes to leave.

Nick Jo . . . Jo. *Please?*

Mr Boyd Actually, Jo, yes I would like you to hear this.

She stops.

Nick, now I want you to know that I respect you deeply. But this whole sorry affair seems to have got us all a little tangled. I wonder whether the best thing here should be that you have a bit of time off. Yes? A bit of time away from the school to cool down.

Nick No . . .

Mr Boyd You need to relax. Maybe go on a holiday.

Nick I don't want to go on a holiday.

Mr Boyd Everybody wants a holiday.

Nick You can't force me out of the school, Mr Boyd.

Mr Boyd But, Nick, you are not well. You're stressed. Ms Fletcher here can attest to that.

Nick I'm not stressed. You said I wasn't stressed. You said I was modern. My phone. Buzzing. Humming fridges. Remember? In our meeting? Mr Boyd, you can't get away with this. You're, you're not only silencing a teacher, you're *excluding* me.

Jo Nick. Maybe we should /

Nick You were there, Mr Boyd. You remember. You were in that room telling me that /

Mr Boyd   / What I remember is that yesterday you came to me complaining about some terrible dreams you were having. And I could see how this anxiety was manifesting itself in your behaviour so I decided to, today, give you a solitary and calming task with the registers. It didn't feel right to have you in a classroom. Then I hear at lunchtime you snuck into an extra maths tutorial despite my clear and well-reasoned desire to keep you away from teaching.

Nick   But, but if I didn't do it then Jessica wouldn't have /

Mr Boyd   / And now this. You've clearly upset Ms Fletcher and you've been, I must say, a little short with me too. So what choice have you left me other than to ask you, politely but firmly, to take a few weeks off?

Nick   Jo.

Jo   Maybe he's right, Nick. You have been having these dreams. Some time off might do you good.

Beat.

Mr Boyd   Now I do believe Duncan is working the gates this evening but I wouldn't want to call him to help us end our meeting. Would I?

Nick   No. It's fine. I'll go. I'm going.

Jo   I'll come with you.

Nick   No. I'll go on my own.

He exits.

Mr Boyd   Goodnight, Nick. Try and get some sleep, poor fellow.

Seven

That night.

Martin's *house.*

Martin   And so I can't let that go, can I?

Chloe   No you can't, Martin.

Martin   And lose face like that? I'd never live it down. You know what I'm saying, don't you, Nick?

Nick   Yeah.

Martin   Yeah you know it. And so I'm stood there and I'm thinking, come on, you old dog. Show them. Fuck them. You've got to, yeah?

Nick   Yeah.

Martin   And so I do it. I get on the bike and I just . . .

Chloe   Just . . .?

Martin   And well I just stack it. Course I do. Completely. I don't know what I'm doing. End up toppling over, right off the bloody slope and I cut my arms all down here and here. In hospital for a week.

Chloe   Oh amazing. How funny, Nick.

Nick   Yeah. Hilarious.

Martin   Thing is though, I showed nerve. And that's what's important. I showed balls. And in life, it's how you act, not how you talk. How are you finding the venison, mate?

Nick   Yeah. Yeah, it's lovely.

Martin   It's what?

Nick   It's lovely, Martin. Really nice.

Martin   What I did was I cooked it in a water bath for about two hours and then finished it off in the pan.

Nick   Right.

Chloe   We were looking at water baths, weren't we?

Nick   Were we?

Chloe   Yes. Thanks for paying attention.

Martin *and* **Chloe** *laugh.*

Nick   I thought all baths were water baths.

Martin   You won't look back, guys. I can promise you that.

Chloe   Don't be silly, Nick.

Nick   I'm not.

Martin   Do you slow-cook very much, Nick?

Nick   Not really.

Martin   Well you will do.

Chloe   Sold. Let's do it.

Nick   I'm not that much of a cook.

Martin   What's that, mate?

Nick   I said I'm not that much of a cook. Don't know what I'd make of a water bath to be honest.

Martin   I don't . . .

Chloe   Well, we can learn. Can't we, Nick? We can learn how to use a water bath.

Nick   We've barely learnt how to use the hob. We're not that into fancy food, Martin. Normally if it's beige and comes in plastic then we'll just have that and what we don't have for dinner we'd have for breakfast. That's how it works round ours. Can I do a pizza in a water bath?

Martin   Well, no.

Chloe   You're being silly, Nick.

Nick   I'm just being honest.

Martin   Nick's hitting on a good point actually. There's nothing wrong with being honest about one's shortcomings.

Nick   Shortcomings?

Chloe   You know, you're right, Martin. We have to admit that we just don't make enough time for the important things.

Nick   Water baths aren't important.

Martin   What's that, mate?

Nick   I said we're busy people, Martin. You know how it is.

Martin   Of course. And how are things going at school, Nick?

Nick   Okay. Yeah. Busy.

Martin   You getting your homework in on time?

Nick   Yeah, yeah. Good one.

Chloe   Things are getting better now, aren't they, Nick?

Nick   Better? What do you mean?

Martin   Chloe told me you've been having some problems.

Nick   She did?

Martin   Depression, Nick. The black dog.

Nick   I'm not depressed.

Martin   And nightmares too. Nasty.

Nick   Chloe?

Chloe   I thought it would help. It was before you said not to. But it's good news now, isn't it? Things are getting better.

Martin   And so I thought, what with Nick getting back in the swing of things and us getting ever so closer to a certain someone's birthday . . . Why don't we throw a bit of a party?

Chloe   A birthday party? You can't!

Martin   Course I don't want to tread on anyone's toes. You hadn't started making plans, had you, Nick?

Nick Started making . . . No, not firm plans no. Ideas, mainly. Keeping it open.

Martin You weren't thinking of taking her out the country, were you?

Nick No.

Martin A weekend away?

Nick No.

Martin A few nights in Paris?

Nick No. I'm . . . Not this year. No.

Chloe We're not really birthday people, Martin.

Martin Everyone's a birthday person, Chloe. What is this, *Angela's Ashes*? You've got to have a birthday party. I was thinking maybe the Grayson.

Chloe The Grayson Hotel? We've always said about a night there, haven't we, Nick?

Nick Yeah.

Martin I thought we could get a band, invite some friends, bring in caterers. Get a fucking planner if we want one.

Chloe We can't get a planner!

Martin Well here I also thought you might want to do it yourself. I know you're like. You'd probably do it better than any of the professionals anyway.

Chloe You know I would enjoy that. I do like to plan, don't I, Nick?

Martin You're a creative spirit. You'd want to be involved. That's why I didn't want it to be a surprise. I hope you don't mind me springing it on you like this, Nick?

Nick What? No. It's just . . .

Martin Just what, mate?

Chloe Just what, Nick?

Nick I mean . . . Oh come on, Chloe, as nice as all this sounds, we can't afford that. It's just not the kind of thing we can do. Is it?

Chloe No, I suppose not.

Martin Nick, you don't understand what I'm saying. I want to do it. As my present to Chloe, to say thank you. And as a gesture to you, mate, after everything you've been through.

Nick You can't do that.

Martin I want to. And want, in this world, is the strongest element known to man. I've never wanted something that I haven't had, Nick.

Chloe Martin, maybe Nick's right. It's too much.

Martin Nothing's too much. Not for us. We've all got decisions to make, Chloe. Every moment, every second, is a crossroads. Do we turn left into obsolescence or do we turn right, to success?

Chloe We turn right, Martin.

Nick *laughs.*

Martin Something the matter, mate?

Chloe What are you sniggering at?

Nick Nothing.

Martin Which way do you turn, Nick?

Nick What's that?

Martin At the crossroads. Which way do you turn?

Nick I think I'm pulling over and asking for directions myself, Martin.

Chloe Nick.

Martin   I wonder if I could be so bold as to offer you a bit of advice, mate?

Nick   Please do.

Martin   Honestly, I've got deep respect for you. Really have. It's good to be resilient. And you're doing great. Don't get me wrong. Teaching, man, someone's got to do it. I just think that the defences you have, the mechanisms you use, can sometimes stifle your ambition. You have to be careful that a cycle of stasis doesn't warp how you see the world, see what people are actually doing for you.

Nick   Stasis. That's your word.

Chloe   It's not my word.

Martin   You're not a lazy person, Nick. I know you're not. And I know how easy it is to get stuck. We've all been there. I see you, mate. I see you.

Nick   You see me?

Martin   I do. It's all about hunger. How hungry are you?

Nick   Not very.

Martin   No?

Nick   Not after two courses of your lovely cooking, no.

Martin   Ah! Funny!

Nick   No. I really take that to heart, Martin. Particularly coming from you. If you can see it then it must be bloody obvious.

Chloe   Nick. Don't be like that.

Nick   How should I be, Chloe?

Martin   Now, pal.

Nick   Pal? Who says pal?

Martin   I think I've said something wrong.

Chloe No you haven't. Nick's just being . . .

Nick What am I being, pal?

Chloe Don't pal me.

Nick He pals me.

Martin Friends . . . Let's not lose the table.

Nick Lose the . . . Jesus, you really are a prick.

Chloe Oh my God.

Nick I mean you must sense it, with the shit that comes out of your mouth. I don't expect anyone who works for you to tell you but you must at least hear yourself, no?

Martin I hear myself, Nick. And trust me, no one takes on my advice more than me. And look at where I've got to. So it can't all be that shit, can it?

Nick No. You know what, you're probably right. But there is one thing. You can't have a cycle of stasis. If it's in a cycle then it's not fucking static, is it?

Beat.

Chloe Have you finished?

Nick Yes. You know what, yes I have.

Part Three

One

The present. Night time.

Nick I see this boy there amongst the History block. He's
lying in the rubble and, and so I rush over and I pull . . . I
pull him up by the, the arm but as I do I hear a kind of rip
. . . and as I pull . . . his body tears in half. And I realise he's
nothing but parts. Wet, hot parts. So I put him down, I try
to, gently. I feel sick but I feel sad too because he's still crying
out to me and I just end up standing there . . . Useless. And
then at that moment a brilliant light pops and blinds me and
I realise it must be a second explosion. I'm flung into the air
and I separate into a million bits. That's when I wake up.
That's when I always wake up. When I'm in a million bits.
And the thing is, I make this happen. I make the whole thing
happen again and again because it only happens if I dream
it. It only happens if I see it. So it's my fault.

Two

Earlier.

The morning.

In the car.

Chloe Don't you care?

Nick Of course I care.

Chloe You completely showed yourself up.

Nick I don't think I said anything unreasonable.

Chloe You were rude to him the whole night.

Nick Come on. He was being a dick.

Chloe   No. The only dick there was you. I can't believe it. I had to sit there listening to you do that to my boss. Do you have any idea how that made me feel?

Nick   He was taking the piss out of me and you know he was. That should bother you. That's the kind of behaviour you should be pissed off with.

Chloe   You're frustrated with your own life so you're lashing out.

Nick   Lashing out? I was telling the truth.

Chloe   You know what the scary thing is? I really think you believe that. I should've seen this coming. We've been in a rut for so long you're scared.

Nick   Scared of what?

Chloe   Everything, Nick. You're scared of everything, you're petrified of change. It's the school that's done this.

Nick   You don't know what you're talking about. It's the likes of Martin, who just plough through life doing fuck-all for anyone else and yet spout such drivel about /

Chloe   / Nick.

Nick   About taking opportunities and crossroads and/

Chloe   / Nick. I'm not talking about Martin anymore.

Nick   There's no point pretending, Chloe. All that kind of thing. It just isn't us.

Chloe   No, Nick. I think it just isn't you.

Beat.

Whatever you've got going on, you need to work it out. Now. I can't stand by and wait anymore. You know that, don't you?

Nick   Pull in here.

Chloe   Where?

Nick Here. I'm going to walk through the park today.

Chloe But it's almost nine.

Nick I know what I'm doing, Chloe.

Three

That lunchtime.

Mrs Nightingale's class.

Jessica *is sat at a desk.*

Nick *enters.*

Nick Hey, sorry I'm late.

Jessica Sir?

Jo *appears.*

Jo Nick. What are you doing here?

Nick What am *I* doing here? What, what are *you* doing here? This is my maths club.

Jo You're not meant to be here, Nick.

Nick Hello, Jessica. What are we working on today?

Jessica Still the fractions, sir.

Jo You have to leave, Nick.

Nick Jo, look, I understand. I really do. I wanted to talk to you and I wanted to explain. I completely really understand why you did what you did and maybe I would have done the same thing too in your position. But the thing is I also think you'd do what I'm doing as well. And the problem is you can't see what I can see and I don't think you really appreciate what's going on here.

Jo We have to talk about this another time, Nick. Not in front of a student.

Jessica   Should I leave, Ms?

Jo   Yes.

Nick   No . . . Jessica, no. We can't keep sheltering these students from what's important.

Jo   I can't lose my job by being associated with you in this.

Nick   That's all you care about, Jo? Your job?

Jo   This is serious shit to me. And if I get sacked because I'm too close to you, or if the school shuts because of your crazy rumour then I'm going to be on my arse. I'm not going to get a job in the academies. I've spent my entire career protesting against them.

Nick   You told Boyd about me doing the maths club yesterday. You ratted me out so it wouldn't look like we're friends.

Jo   Nick, I care about you but I can't let you destroy other people's lives for this. You shouldn't be in the building. If you go now then I won't tell Boyd. I don't even know why you'd risk it. I don't even know why you're here.

Nick   I'm here to ask for help.

Jo   Well I've told you. I can't help you in the way you need.

Nick   I don't mean help from you.

Jessica *stands*.

Jessica   I believe in you, sir.

Jo   Jessica.

Jessica   I believe in you, sir! The truth! We need the truth!

Jo   Jessica, get out. Now.

Jessica   No.

Jo   Jessica Havens, I will have you suspended.

Jessica *leaves*.

Jo Are you determined to rip this place apart? Whose help were you after, Nick? Don't tell me you've told any of the students.

Nick I've got to stop this, Jo. That's what my dreams mean. It's up to me. It always has been. The bombs are going. And then once they've gone, once there are no bombs, then there won't be any more dreams either. Don't you see? Getting rid of the bombs will stop everything.

Jo If you don't leave now I will call the police. Nick, this is it. This has to be it.

Four

That evening?

At home.

Nick Chloe? Hello? Chloe, it's me. Look, I suppose we should chat.

Martin *enters.*

Martin Nick.

Nick Martin?

Martin Sorry, mate, I didn't realise you were coming over. I've only put enough in for two.

Nick Put enough in of what? Why are you here?

Martin I suppose I could quickly chuck in another bit. The water bath's only just kicking up.

Nick Water bath? What are you talking about? What are you doing here?

Martin How was school?

Nick Fine. But I don't /

Martin / Any homework?

Nick   Martin, is Chloe home?

Martin   I'm sure she'll be down in a minute.

Nick   Down?

Martin   Are you ok, mate? You're looking tired.

Nick   I didn't expect to see you here.

Martin   What did you expect?

Nick   What?

Martin   What did you expect? Really?

Nick   I expected to talk to Chloe. We've got a lot of things to talk about.

Martin   You're a good man, Nick. You're one of life's good guys.

Nick   Why do you say that?

Martin   Because it's true. And it's sad because you know more than anyone that being good doesn't mean that you win.

Nick   Win what? What are you talking about? Where's Chloe? Chloe?

Chloe *enters.*

Chloe   Nick.

Nick   What's going on? Why's Martin here?

Chloe   What do you mean *why's Martin here*, why the hell are you here?

Nick   What?

Chloe   You can't just expect to waltz back in here, Nick. You get out of the car one morning and I don't see you for a week.

Nick   A what? A week?

Chloe   The fuck were you playing at?

Martin   You do smell a bit, mate. Smells like the park.

Nick   What are you talking about? I've been out for a day.

Chloe   I was worried sick.

Nick   I went to the school and then I walked right back. It's the same fucking day, Chloe.

Martin   Now don't get angry, pal.

Nick   And this. What the fuck is this about? I mean I say a day and you say a week but it's still a bit fucking quick to start an affair.

Martin   Start?

Chloe   Nick, it's only an affair if there was still love in the relationship.

Nick   That's not the dictionary definition, Chloe. Where's all my stuff?

Chloe   Your van collected it.

Nick   What?

Chloe   We put your stuff out. A van collected it right away. We thought that was you.

Nick   When have I ever mentioned to you about owning a fucking van, Chloe?

Martin   Are you succumbing to dark thoughts, Nick?

Nick   What?

Martin   Do you feel as though you are being crushed to liquid?

Nick   What? Where did you /

Chloe   / Jo rang three days ago asking about you. You didn't tell me you'd been suspended.

Nick   I'm not suspended. I'm on holiday.

Martin   Nice holiday.

Nick   What?

Chloe   Have you spoken to her?

Martin   To a dark liquid, mate. I see you. I see you.

Nick   Chloe, Martin's really pissing me off.

Chloe   Can you go and get Nick a glass of water please, Martin?

Martin   Course.

He exits.

Nick   Why he's getting me water from my own fucking kitchen. That's my water, Chloe. He doesn't even know where the glasses are.

Chloe   He knows where the glasses are, Nick. I don't want you getting angry.

Nick   I'm not angry.

Chloe   We all just need to keep calm.

Nick   I am calm. I'm fucking calm, Chloe.

Chloe   We were just at a crossroads . . . And you went one way and I went . . . the other.

Nick   Chloe, if you knew, if you had any idea about the things that are going on right now . . . Everything's changed. The bombs have changed everything.

Chloe   What bombs? What are you talking about?

Nick   I never wanted this. I never wanted any of it. I just want everything to go back to the way it was.

Chloe   But the way it was doesn't exist anymore. And that's a good thing. Isn't it?

Martin *comes back with a glass of water.*

Chloe Why don't you have some water, Nick?

Nick I don't want any fucking water.

Martin Hey, don't get aggressive about the water, mate.

Nick It's not the water, Martin. It's the fucker holding it.

Martin Look I think it's time we called it a night, hey?

Nick Yes, I think that's a good idea. Thanks, Martin.

Beat.

Oh what, you mean for *me* to call it a night? For me to go?

Martin I think it's for the best, pal. Don't you?

Nick Chloe?

Chloe Think of this as an opportunity, Nick. To start again.

Nick Chloe, I really need you to understand because I'm about to do something incredible. The bombs, Chloe. I'm going to get rid of the bombs.

Martin It's nice to have a project.

Chloe Nick, you have so much potential. It's what I fell in love with in the first place. Some day you're going to find yourself again. We're all going to be proud of you.

Nick The bombs.

Chloe So proud.

Five

That night. The present.

The moment after **Nick** *has finished his monologues.*

The Brink.

Nick And so that's it. That's the dream. And every night I go through the same pattern, stuck in this cycle where I'm helpless. But I'm not helpless in real life. Am I?

Jessica *appears. We realise it is her he has been talking to in the present.*

Jessica I don't think so, sir.

Nick But I can't help thinking that if I hadn't have had the dreams then maybe they wouldn't exist. If I hadn't have known about it then maybe it would never explode.

Jessica But it still would've been down there. Except no one would have known except Boyd.

Nick Boyd and, and the government. Remember the government.

Jessica Yes. So you needed to have the dreams, you needed the dreams to save us, sir.

Nick Yes. Yes, you're right. But please call me Nick.

Jessica Nick. I had to lie to my mum tonight. She asked where I was going and I didn't know what to say. What *are* we doing out here, sir . . . I mean, Nick.

Nick Don't you see? This is it. And, and you told me to tell the truth. Well this is the truth. And we're going to end it. Me and you.

Jessica How? Are you going to get Mr Boyd arrested?

Nick What? No.

Jessica Then what are you going to do?

Nick Underneath us here, Jessica, are the bombs. My dreams, all of this, has been leading me to here. And I'm going to dig them up.

He picks up a spade and starts digging.

Bright spotlights. The sound of a helicopter. The sound of trucks.

Jessica *runs away.*

Mr Boyd (*in a megaphone, off*)   Get away! Get out of the way!

Nick   Stop! Wait! I'm a teacher!

Mr Boyd (*in a megaphone, off*)   Out of the way!

Nick   Mr Boyd? You're blinding me.

Mr Boyd *enters.*

Mr Boyd   Nick, what the hell are you doing?

Nick   Mr Boyd, am I dying?

Mr Boyd   Of course you're not. You shouldn't be here.

Nick   What's going on?

Mr Boyd   This isn't safe for you, Nick. You need to leave.

Nick   What are all these people doing?

Mr Boyd   They're digging up the bombs.

Nick   I'm digging up the bombs.

Mr Boyd   No, Nick. No, you're not. You weren't here. You saw none of this.

Nick   I need to do this.

Mr Boyd   Oh mark my words, Nick. You are central to events here. This is all happening because of you. You spooked them, you've worried them. And they've always been troubled, Nick. They're troubled people at the best of times. The *tempers* . . . I wanted to get that across to you. There are going to be repercussions, I've been told to tell you that. I'm sorry.

Nick   Look at them, Mr Boyd. Look at how many of them there were. Seeing them out of the ground, I'm already feeling so much better.

Mr Boyd   Incredible, isn't it?

Nick   What are they going to do with the hole?

Mr Boyd   You don't need to know that. You don't need to know anything anymore, Nick.

Nick   I've really done it, haven't I, Mr Boyd? I've really messed with the order of things.

Mr Boyd   You had the fear of a young man in you. Inspiring, in a way. I'm sorry I didn't protect you.

Nick   What should I do now, Mr Boyd? I can't go home.

Mr Boyd   Nick, I don't think there's very much you can do. What you seem to have done throughout this whole sorry affair is gradually and systemically limit your choices down to one.

Nick   Jessica? Do you mean Jessica?

Mr Boyd   I mean your exit.

Nick   The park. I could go to the park.

Mr Boyd   Nick, wait.

Nick *exits.*

Six

The next day. Thursday morning.

The park.

Nick *wakes up on the ground. Student* **One** *is stood over him.*

One   Sir . . .? Sir . . .? Are you ok, sir?

Nick   What's going on?

One   You were asleep, sir.

Nick   What?

One   You were asleep in the park, sir. Shit.

Nick Don't fuss. And don't swear. Help me find my shoe.

They look.

Have you ever seen the sun rise over the buildings there? It makes such a beautiful shape. It's like they're designed like that on purpose. For that moment right there. And we're having it now. You and me.

Beat.

What do you want?

One Nothing.

Nick What do you mean *nothing*? Got to want something. What are you doing?

One I just saw you lying there, sir. I'm on my way to school.

Nick To school?

One Here's where I meet my girlfriend. Are you ok, sir? Do you need me to get you someone?

Nick What? No. I'm fine. I'm good. I'm great. Waking up for once in a really good mood. Look at the sky. So bright. Come on.

One Come on?

Nick Don't want to be late. I'll walk with you.

One Late for what?

Nick School, you dumbo! Don't want to start your day with a black mark, do you?

One Jess isn't here yet, sir.

Nick What?

One My girlfriend isn't here yet, sir. Here's where I meet her.

Nick What did you say, what's her name?

One   Jessica Havens, sir. You know her, sir. She's in your maths club.

Nick   Is Jessica really your, your girlfriend?

One   Yes, sir.

Nick   Surely you're too young.

One   We've not done full sex, if that's what you're /

Nick   / No, I mean you're too young *for her*. You're just a boy.

One   We're in the same class, sir.

Nick   She never said.

One   Said what?

Nick   She never told me she had a boyfriend.

One   Why would she, sir?

Nick   Why?

One   Yeah.

Nick   Because we tell each other everything.

One   I love her, sir.

Nick   No, you don't. Don't be . . . You don't even understand what that means.

One   You don't know that, pal.

Nick   Hey, don't call me pal.

One   You don't think she loves Matthew Timms, do you, sir?

Nick   What?

One   Matthew Timms, sir. You don't think she loves him, do you, sir? Because he started a rumour that he fingered her behind the bins behind the English block but I couldn't hit him because it was before we were going out and because it wasn't true. Sir.

Nick No she doesn't love Matthew Timms.

One Oh good.

Nick She loves me.

One What?

Nick She doesn't love Matthew Timms and she doesn't love you. She loves me.

One *starts to laugh in disbelief.*

One Sir?

Nick Why are you laughing? Stop laughing.

One I'm sorry, Nick.

Nick Don't call me Nick.

One Come on, pal. It was a joke!

Nick I told you to stop calling me pal.

One You're stressed. You've got to sleep, Nick. Sleep's important for a healthy brain.

Nick I see what this is. I see what you are.

One I'm just a student, sir.

Nick You're *them* and you're here to crush me into a liquid. Well, it's too late. You can do what you like but the truth is it's over. The bombs are gone. I stopped it.

One Then why's it still ticking?

Nick What?

One Tick tick tick.

He laughs uncontrollably.

Nick   Stop laughing, don't laugh at me. Hey, stop it. Shut up. Shut up. Come here.

He lunges at **One**. *Grabs him by the collar.*

One   This may manifest itself into a headache.

Blackout.

A moment.

Lights rise.

Jessica *is stood alone. She is sobbing.*

We see **Nick**'s *back. He is hunched into a bush.*

Jessica   What have you done? What have you done?

Nick *stands. His front is covered head to toe in blood.*

Nick   Jessica.

Jessica   I can't believe you've done this.

Nick   We have to get out of here, Jessica. We have to go right away.

Jessica   No.

Nick   No? What . . .

Jessica   I can't believe you've . . . You've gone too far, sir.

Nick   How can you say that? It was . . . That wasn't real, Jessica. That wasn't . . . That was *them*.

Jessica   He was my *boyfriend*, Nick.

Nick   What? No, he . . . You never told me you had a boyfriend.

Jessica   Why would I tell you?

Nick   Because we told each other the truth.

Jessica   I don't think we can talk anymore. My mum says.

Nick   Don't be silly. Why are you being silly?

Jessica I shouldn't have come with you to the Brink last night. She's angry with me, sir.

Nick Hey, come on. Call me Nick.

Jessica I don't want to call you Nick anymore.

Nick Don't say that.

Jessica You're in a lot of trouble, sir. You're in a lot of trouble now.

Nick I don't care.

Jessica But you have to.

Nick Why?

Jessica Because you're an adult. You have to be an adult otherwise we can't be children. And if no one teaches us properly now then how can we ever be grown-ups?

Nick I told you the truth.

Jessica But it meant something different to you, sir.

Further into the park.

The world is disintegrating.

Mr Boyd *is there.*

Mr Boyd Look alive, Nick.

Nick Yes, trying to. They came for me, Mr Boyd. And I didn't take it. I stood up for myself.

Mr Boyd What?

Nick Them. They came for me. Because of the bomb. And . . . and they weren't expecting me to fight back.

Mr Boyd No, Nick. They haven't come for you yet.

Nick But that was . . .

Mr Boyd That was just a student.

Nick   Oh.

Mr Boyd   There's going to be a lot of paperwork, Nick. A lot of paperwork, indeed.

Nick   What happens now?

Mr Boyd   Now? Now you've hurt a student, now they come for you.

Nick   Did they mean for that to happen, did they . . . Was Jessica . . . Mr Boyd, I'm confused.

Mr Boyd   Think of a cup, Nick. And think of pouring water into that cup. And you're pouring and pouring and pouring until the cup is full. And if you don't stop pouring. What happens?

Nick   You make a mess.

Mr Boyd   You make a mess. And that's what this is. This is a mess.

Nick   You know there's one thing I wish I did differently. I wish I listened more to people who didn't think they knew what they were on about. They tell us so much, every day. I wish I listened more to doubt. Can I ask you something?

Mr Boyd   Anything, Nick.

Nick   Was I a good teacher, Mr Boyd?

Mr Boyd   You just might be the very worst teacher I have ever laid my eyes on, Nick.

A bolt of light flashes across the park.

A cacophony of noise (a chorus of angels?) lifts **Nick** *into the air before he separates into a million pieces.*

End